OF DUST AND SPARROWS

To Harriet and Josephine

and Antoinette, Patricia,
Elaine and Cindy

They did not imitate any living
thing.

Robert Hazel

*Contemporaries*
Robert Hazel, Editor

# OF DUST AND SPARROWS

by
Arthur Sappé

New York University Press
New York     1970

# CONTENTS

| | |
|---|---|
| A Seascape | 7 |
| A Dialogue of Greek Gods and Progeny | 9 |
| Birds Again | 12 |
| Mist | 16 |
| The Suburbs | 18 |
| The Leopard | 19 |
| On William Blake | 21 |
| Dust of My City | 22 |
| Question | 23 |
| Age is . . . | 24 |
| The Chant | 25 |
| Elegy | 27 |
| Origin of a God | 28 |
| Departure | 30 |
| The Absentee Father | 31 |
| My Aunt | 47 |
| Question | 48 |
| A Sextet of Voices | 49 |
| The Poet Laureate | 55 |
| Cockeral | 57 |
| Moab's Soliloquoy | 59 |
| Morning | 61 |

# A SEASCAPE

Not listed in the World Almanac
nor in a Strange Catalogue

Watch the water . . .

and all about it . . .

We are a salt solution
with a sprinkle of minerals.

What are nipples and hair

Sheepshead are ninety-two percent liquid.

The hidden narrator chirps and points
with thumbs plugged into callous waves
in a careless seascape.

"Without consent for warm customers
I will describe the soiled face of our mobile stage.
Everywhere there are pink signals and sonatas
Scarlet signs from impacted suns
and hollow volcanoes.
There are protests but no answers to color and heat."

Aloofly and loftily calls caw caw
the morning tinted gull
between gulps of sky with a blue tounge
Honk Honk the crane argues
in an angular silhouette.

The society snipe squeaks
Oh me, who taunts the tern.

Lap, lap gurgle the water peeps
The transparent wind complains with invisible whistle.
Yaw Yaw the pilings rub
Like cumbersome and defeated brothers

The awkward pelican without etiquette flaps
The bubbles pop in the wave froth
and the sand is fractured to grits
while the fiddler crab clicks a rondo
of dissent.

And the beach imitates
a drunken and exhausted stockbroker
costumed in tennis white
Who splashes into the nervous ocean

Mother of compulsive clams
and periwinkle shells.

# A DIALOGUE OF GREEK GODS AND PROGENY*

Zeus to Hera:
    "I will be with them always

                but they are an affliction
Whales
    and cactus
        in heat
        Why did we not burn whips
        Puncture pacifiers
        Leave intact fetters and shackles
                in the wet of afternoons
*Not mentioned by Bullfinch but fortunately
excavated on a nameless island north of Crete.


We tarried
        behind
           a blueberry bush
On
        compliant
          and intricate moss
Respect for ant piles
        and feckless bears
             are not for us.
    Mincing, drudging and begging
    In arenas of muck

    They no longer entertain
    the pulp and mannikins
    of man

    And less for reckless and fluid
    children.
             Puberty blends
             with mockery and
             arrogance

The litany
        is clad
            in a carnival
                of rebellion
With fountain
            tongues
                uncircumcised
                    pipe high
                        with ridicule
Quick biting is the peach pit.
            Bitterness is forgotten.
                        Listen to their scherzo snap."
The children, clothed in long hair, wiggle:

"Right you are mommy and daddyoo
Supercorrect.
RAZZLE DAZZLE DELTA PI NOT NOT
WE ARE THE SIBLINGS FROM A FLOWER POT
                Cord maple kindle into spits
                Orange coals transform crackles
                Blaze hydrogen, flame liquid oxygen
Incinerate alfalfa
                and needles of pine
                    Equal fire for comfort
                        of jangling bones and twitches

Nervous vines for hands
                scalp itches
                Sparky eyes
                elastic feet
Urges naive and indiscreet
Swirling spines
                Tingling water
                Conception light
                    for skepticism."

The children's reply is a freshet of voices
lightening lips unchewed by teeth of glass:
"RAZZLE DAZZLE DELTA PI NOT NOT
WE ARE THE SIBLINGS FROM A FLOWER POT"

Hera to Zeus:

"Do not be impatient or abrupt.
Mandrake anticipates the sun.
The young search for identity
in   frolic.

Let them catch a caterpillar
Knot the flaps
and build fallible empires
in "tents of blood and butter."

# BIRDS AGAIN

We are wingless birds
on empty islands
surrounded by exits.
  We squat on saw grass and macadam
unaware of our windless glide
from inverted images
frozen in a welter sea of kelp
to the drunken bottoms of mirrors.
  Silver and water do not reflect
they distort lives and leaves
and the hollow plumage
of staid sea gulls
carved from steel
with a random stroke.

  Apparitions do not spring
from the green skirted
dances of humble marigolds
or the suspicious forefingers of a child
They covort in mushroom caves
and tarry on meadows of tar
reserved for the naps of limousines.

  They are floating half submerged darts
in a slow hallway
girdled by oak bannisters
screwed to wounded rooms
crawling to basements of dust
with the cadence of ancient dialogues
grated among the murmuring of starlings
and kiss of floor slabs
laced and trampled
by the raven's fetish.

The peasant, the pervert
and the embroidered pope
gingerly clambor the scaffold
gird their nates
condemn followers and kin
and are content
to gurgle and be fulfilled
at the snap of a blade.
Vibration and motion are constant
Conversation does not end
    nor cunning.
They descend into poetry.

THE SPARROW CHIRPS A WARNING NOT A MELODY
AND HIS KISS IS NOT A REWARD BUT AN EXILE.

The pelican in the supermarket
wheels the galvanized cart
shaking with mixed frozen fish.
He shops for himself and not for me.
The awkward and silly bird
with a pound of amber-gris
to barter for time in a shaker bottle
with a magic screw off lid
and a sack of orange candles;
but the shelves were empty.
    The grocer re-ordered only important items.
He was addled by the formless music
of ripped apple crates
vibrating lettuce heads
blowing asparagus
and rubbing ears of corn.

THE SPARROW CHIRPS A WARNING NOT A MELODY
AND HIS KISS IS NOT A REWARD BUT AN EXILE.

We learn with clumsy hammers
located beyond our senses

13

And squat mothers
little Mrs. Continuity
self appointed and accidental
watch bitch at the vaults
of flesh and tradition
with a cord
half nutrition, part tether
and knotted to me
despite the recent chop of a granite ax.

But when we asked
you answered with a scream and a sigh
your blue egg was cracked
and you released me
from the pink chowder
of the pregnancy farm.

With your halter secure
you allowed us to sing,
our brains to wander,
stole our bubble gum wrappers
and ripped the favorite toy drum,
drove us into the monkey bars
of the deserted park
to dissolve into loneliness.

THE SPARROW CHIRPS A WARNING NOT A MELODY
AND HIS KISS IS NOT A REWARD BUT AN EXILE.

Child father in your confirmation suit
clutching a commutation ticket
and untrained sister
spun into a cacoon of wax and shingles
of a sterilized house temple.
Why do you become as drowsy as caterpillar
at the sound of words?
Where are the dinner guests?

Where has my brother gone
with empty satchels
lean portmanteaus
and calico cats;
with bank book crutches
and monacles
the eye brows
and the hooked beak of owls.
Did they catch the rattling nine fifteen?
    Certainly Mr. Artist
did not follow Mr. Judge along the street;
and what about Mr. Barber?
Did they listen in the station?
Did they ask for a transfer?

THE SPARROW CHIRPS A WARNING NOT A MELODY
AND HIS KISS IS NOT A REWARD BUT AN EXILE.

# MIST

The mist is
a silhouette of forgotten temples
drifting blurred and free
where fetishes of starlight
are danced
within a shock of birches.

An unmarked and flexible cat
pursuing forever a white reckless mouse
pinned to an unpainted landscape.

A confident sea gull
skimming the foam of waves
for the broken bellies of kilifish.

A chaste swan
hiding in the silver reflections
of drowned sun light.

Pale trains coasting on gleaming tracks.

Hobo clouds blown to beg
hills of mashed potatoes
from the hollow of a porcelain bowl.

The smoke of dead leaves
unburned in the corridors of a hospital
tended by tumors and grey nuns.

The tail of a snow rabbit
disappearing under the staves of a bleached fence.

A faded woman
fondling a necklace
between starched sheets and a ripped pillow case.

16

It is a conclave of old men
in long underwear shearing sheep.

And the mist is the wet dust of myself
and a moth
returning to an interrupted sleep.

# THE SUBURBS

The day sleeps late
criticized by nervous sparrows
the country dressed
in urban clothes
screams of child pains.
the finger grass
folds before
the deaf temple of the wind.
On the road's edge
in endless cubes
the girls play house
and the vetch
has conquered the dandelion.

The seagull drops
clam shells on the macadam
and fights with car tires
for his meal.
The beach
gelded by beer cans
sulks beside
the oil slick bay
deserted by the mullet
and awaits with the passive
motion of water
the conquering dust
of the city.

## THE LEOPARD

The shards of shattered wind shields
a stillborn child
and cracked tubes of fly wings
sprinkle dots on a butter suit
to decorate
the dilemma and exile
of modern man
snared between wives, wars and ash trays
who
sky ride the
cabled winged stallions
of golden elevators
with leggy girls
in leavened black
without a lily of the valley
or a robin
in the bodice.

He returns
terrified by the bells of ether
and under the prurient sun
dreams he is an orange leopard
with asbestos paws
padding the dry troughs
of wind buried water-ways
and vaginal gullies
protected by strands of impertinent cactus
grits of glass sand
and granite tumors.

Instinctively thirsty
he lopes with the memory
of forgotten generations
pursued by souffles of dust
over a reluctant and aggressive desert.

Exhausted at dusk
he shivers
on an angry and dedicated train
propelled by coal mice
seething in the firebox of its stomach
grinding with ambition
to flap pigeons
from arbitrary and grey stations
to his wooden lair
scouring its porch and eaves
against the bark of maple trees.

He has stalked on scarred cordovan boots
barbed wire offices
mushrooms of tar
cinder blocks
frigid temples
and saffron jungle paths
guided by a suspicious
and rigid stray gene
donated by a generous father
who discharged
a revelation of swallows
from a careless sling.

The cubs of the leopard
with coral eyes
sparks for legs
taut whiskers and snouts
pipe and snarl welcomes
abandon tail games
attack his pigskin briefcase
and gullet
the overflowing warm
fresh killed meat of the day.

# ON WILLIAM BLAKE

It was written
in watercolor
with paint smears

         I MISS THEE
         MORE THAN
         THE THINGS
         I SING ABOUT.

         WHERE ARE YOU GOING
         STRAIGHT LINE
         OF TIME;
         FROM THE NEVER WAS
         TO THE NO MORE,
         EXISTING WITHOUT BEING
         AND UNAFFECTED
         BY COMMAS AND EVENTS?

The dog noses
with bowed head
the surface of the earth

A woman screams
a pearl is missing
and that now
her necklace
is incomplete.

And in the long hall
beside our room
the clock chimes . . . . . . . . .
nine times.

# DUST OF MY CITY

There can be seen
solid black dust
between the layers
of wet sand
and the growing earth.

Puffs of dust
from the wheels
of an automobile
on a country road.

Spacial dust
blue charged
and agitated
spinning
new planets.

And in the long afternoon
of my city
still the quiet dust
over the pink cathedral
descends
to sleep among
the hoboes
on Bleeker Street.

# QUESTION

Did the wry sparrow
ever sleep in a cold cathedral
or in a court yard of hair?

Did I doze
or did I see a wing
flutter from an iron fence
and vanish into a cross of elm trees?

# AGE IS...

Age is
toe
and fingernails
sucked up
by a vacuum

A tooth spit
with celery
on a parquet floor
and swallowed
by a hungry dog

A tennis racquet
and merit badge
burned
to kindle maple leaves

A gray hair
retrieved by a sparrow
and woven
into a nest
with cigar bands

# THE CHANT

Prisoners
bound in red brick
reinforced
with hardened concrete
and caked dust

The owl andirons
in the fireplace
from orange exile
among chips
and slabs
of Douglas fir
and Sitka spruce
sing fire songs

Anticipating
their release to burn
distant pale ferns
loose eels
in grass tunnels
and country sparrows
in briar topped tents
and the ruin of temporary cities
of plaster walls
window glass
and the empty people
surrounding all
Singing
burn, burn
to living things
singing
burn, burn
to dead things

Owls in the fireplace
singing in unison
burn, burn
to everything

# ELEGY

On basalt nights
between star spears
and meadow saffron
bitter palominos
in cinnamon
and white
roam
the same
passive salt grass
where naked
but for beads
and shells
splinters
of Indian children
played
at
survival games
and
lost

# ORIGIN OF A GOD

In the block panelled
room of a solid house
on the side of a hill
overlooking the river
built by a Quaker
to harbor negroes
during the war;
in a carved maple chair
on a
loomed in England rug
saturated with dust;
He sat

or so they thought
those who by the iron hinged door
while singing with banjoes
feasting on stuffed pork
and drinking
minted white wine
to celebrate
the protection of the plants
for a prosperous crop
and to place presents
at His feet

but the door was bolted shut
and the thick copper key
many generations ago
had corroded away
and its inaccurate duplicate
served
these people;
His followers
in blue denim
and organdy

it was later when
the exhausted but happy revelers
wandered through the Ohio hills
to their white homes
leaving in the dark hallway
leading to His door
a tame crow
a jar of honey
a jug of whiskey
a crock of mincemeat
and a handmade guitar
in His chamber
there was silence
and motionless He collected
of these gifts.

# DEPARTURE

                    No longer
in the troughs of heaven
do the wings of sparrows
drink light.

                    It is a dark island
inhabited by aphids and moles,
black flecked palominos freed
and the pale bodies of memories
                    are borne
                    by wimpled women
and secreted in the corridors of the mind.
                    Lost boys
                    spanked by loneliness
                    cry out, whimper
and rock in confused circles
mourning their thirsty houses.

# THE ABSENTEE FATHER

A Poem in Play Form

### The Father

There is nothing before him.
He has been with us always
with unseen light
a part of us.
The owner of space
in a small borrowed room
awakens
stretches the curtains
and in an artificial nite
removes a rug
woven for him
by his mother
with hook
carved for her
by her father
of locust wood
and wool
carded by his sister.
He bores with an electric drill
three small holes
into the linoleum floor
and thru the ceiling
of the restaurant below.
One for his eye
one for his ear
and a slanted one
for his finger.

## The Cook

He with remarkable hands
who came to prepare
the corpses of sorrel
and rabbits,
protector of the fire
and the utensils
of the food ceremony,
shells peas
like time pellets
in his lap.
Three outcasts of the sun
from light and heat—
other things,
a man a woman a child
sit and sip fetish water.
All are aware
but not sure,
ferns leaning toward light,
that someone is peering
at them
and listening.
They stare at the blue ceiling
inhabited by peeling white
plaster planets
above a revolving fan.
But they see nothing.

## The Mother

In my house
all things grow well.
I am the mint of it all,
the keeper of the stamps
and tradition, of birth,
of continuity.
My round land
soft and secure
with green hair
moves quietly
on its precise journey
creating answers
and evolving a fig.
My poetry is for living things.
Why do you not listen
to me?
I am these things
and know them well.
You are too slow.
The beetle in bronze chains
cannot reach
the rotted tree.
The caterpillar discovers
his wings too late
and the chaste seagull
dies like any bird.
Be fast as seasons,
the surf,
the boulders dislodged
by moss.
Oil comes from seed
only when pressed.

Listen
I saw two rocks
in the architecture of a desert
and a cloud,
a dream
in a sea of sand,
sitting side by side
in a unique
and particular way,
independent as Eskimos
waiting for a mouse.
And in shaped arguments
saying
Time is the present
hiding and successful
as our ancestors
eating raw meat
in a cave,
killed by a stone ax.

## The Cook

I have no time for this.
Women are too close to fire.
You are prone to the smoke
in hallways and canals,
to brushfires in canyons,
the pall of sewers,
the haze of space.
I will turn my back
on your sky,
a hump of silence.

# The Thief

I am not interested in tender ears
or the shaded eye of time.
The dog drips saliva
before the kill,
the hawk swings low
and the soldier cries.
In this dark land
I came to steal
as suspicious as
someone in history.
I wet my diaper
and I live to kiss it.
I do not like to do this.
If there was a choice
I would have ridden horses.
My mother liked stallions
and my father bays.
I'll take the yellow
from the blue
and kill the green giant.
I hate the endless trees
growing in a straight line
and marching with turtles
to oblivion.
Put down your water
and your food.
No one will worship
until my business is done.

## The Cook

Into the shodding shop
I came without shoes,
with the glow
of stripped mahogany
wet, red wrinkled
and unafraid
to prepare the way for others.
Put your green gun
and the Bible
between the salt shakers.
You have no need for them here.
We have so little
for you to steal.

## The Child

How strange you look,
a broken clam shell
in the onyx night
with a kidney for a face,
nervous vines
for arms and legs
and a damp matchbox
for a brain.
Take what you want.
It will become
only an accumulation
of yourself.
Take it all.
You have time
this time.

## The Mother

You are something
to go up
and never come down.
My eyelashes
are above my teeth.
Why don't you take
a bay wind
and leave the fingergrass grow straight?
Take the tides
and let the crabs drown.
Steal the wind
so the cloud
can hang motionless.
Remove the driver
from the car,
the mite
from the parasite,
or the emotion
from the act.
Or is it the child you want?

## The Cook

Take the money.
It does not belong to me.
Silver coins are not permanent.
The coffee grounds from the sink,
the garbage from the can
save the barge
a trip to the sea
and rob the fishes.
Take the green ledger.
It is not heavy.
Everything that has happened
is recorded in it.

# The Thief

I do not want these things.
I did not come for this.
Who wants your child
or anyone else's?
Just let her go.
She is young
and can walk in the park
and tell us
what she has seen
with her tongue
uncut by tin cans.
Maybe my song is elsewhere.

## The Child

I will go, Mother.
I came only because you
were here—
with my belly-button
part yours
To make me pretty
I will
feel the dust in my hands,
play with sparrows,
wind your clock
and put your thread away.
I will twirl and twirl
the silver bracelets
until my wrists are hot
and catch the springtime
in my hair.

## The Thief

Among the vines of decay
in the ashes of old cities
the obsessed cat
crouches by his hole
and does not sleep.
It is a long wait
and he will never hear
the clock of wooden blocks
on the empty streets.
But don't be critical.
His limited weapon
is patience
and it will fail him.
He is not contrite.
The testament of the testicle
dictates action,
will parch the confessional.

## The Child

I tell you with
the opinion of lemon peels.
And I watched the old priest
with dry hands
and a bronze cross
in a dark grove of maples
poking last year's leaves
with his walking stick.
In the brown
he found
a pair of girl's pink underwear,
a medal
from World War II
and a broken
picture tube.
I saw my dust resting
on an iron fence,
my sparrow asleep
in the cathedral
and my song was stilled
by the vibrations of a city.
I watched a bee
sting a city man
and return to his home
with blood on his wings.

## The Father

The renter of the room above
lying
pulls out his fingers
and with his lips close
to the slotted hole
yells:
Don't listen to them,
only to me.
Wails:
Don't hear
their deft calls of coming,
their new song.
Screams:
Listen only to me.
I am the green.
I am part of this.
I have always been here.
Listen only to me.

## The Cook

Who remembers his father
or his father
with his heavy walk
and stout smell?
I do not remember mine.
He left to buy an apple
and six cans of beer,
saying:
You will remember me always—
And I have not seen him since—
The cook puts a coin
with the head of a girl
pressed on it
into the empty slot,
pulls the lever
and as the turntable revolves
the refugees from heat
gathered in the restaurant
turn their heads
toward the music
and they hear
and see
nothing
from the blue ceiling
with plaster planets in it.

# MY AUNT

My aunt
has gone
to buy
a turtle
so she
can carve
her birthdate
upon it.

She says
if they
crawl
as slowly
as they
are supposed to
it will be
a long time
before
the next one.

# QUESTION

Who knows
the secret place?

The underside
of a fern

A spider's trace
Or where a feather
touches the wing
of a sparrow

Dust
on corduroy
Or the top step
leading to the roof
of a tenement
A sound's end?

Who among us
has seen
a cat die

Or understand
a cactus
flower

# SEXTET OF VOICES—
## A Recitative

CHORUS:

WHEN DID THE LIGHT BEGIN?
WHO STRUCK THE MATCH?
WHEN DOES AN ORGASM BEGIN?
WHO MAKES THE CALL?
WHO ANSWERS THE BELL?
WHICH VOICE FROM A DISTANCE REPLIES?
AND SAYS?

## I

"My house was made of warm stone
but my children were always hungry.
    What a strange little child
my son, to go and kill for his mother.
    Do all sons do that?"
    "My journey is too much
the elm tree beside the house is dead."
    "The sparrows washed by summer rain
to help their trip
flew from the tree
to the house
and perched on my father's back
they were unafraid to do this."
    "I did only what I had to
I have things to do right now
I have listened and watched all day
    But you may return
If you wish
to your warm brownstone house
chalked white
by the thousands of fingers
of city moon children
singing the dumplings are done
but the oxtails are not."

## II

"In Ohio the barbarian
tends his pigs all day
and eats them at night
These keepers of the flesh vault
are unknown to the patient
on an oak bench in a hospital
who stands up to step on a roach
and exalted with the
emerging idea screams
If you can talk
You can sleep,
and give a kiss to Harriet
and ask her
If I would have waited
and perhaps stayed too late
until the sky became
an orange candle
beside her
in morning sleep
Would she have been content
to be silent on a stairway
looking only
for window sun?"

"In the dark land
The carbon leaf
of a milkweed
like a black
pinwheel
a toy gift
from a popcorn box
stuck
in a stone fence
in a brisk east wind
watched

by passerine birds
   spins and spins
and everyone fights time."

### III

"The scars and skins
of chrysanthemums
are measured in morality
happiness, gin and lesbians."
   "Go to sleep now and dream
you are an elm tree
with your branches
all over me.
   With a candle and hammer
by your side
magnetized by astral pulls
rock  rock
your maternal womb
and transpose
the mourning of a planet
and the mourning
of a warm child
for the evening of a person
confused by the endless
versions of truth."
   "The best aphrodisiac
is a man or a woman.
It is a personal visit
with spermatozoa
wrapped in a dirty sock
to kill an egg."
   "The women talk of entrance
and men of penetration."

## IV

"Drink the water and listen
it is not a weapon
but a refuge."
"The song is behind the cloud
and the pebble beneath your feet
The silent housewife
and the sparrow
sing to you from the warm house
in the strong forms
of ancient sculpture.
They do not sing
in the unknown
of sand buildings
sea horses and nettle shells
of dog all smell and mouth
and children playing in the hallway
getting close to living things
just to listen
and drink the water
and let the leaves
fall from the elm tree."

# V

"The lakes inhabit the valleys
with islands of women
and shore temples built
and destroyed by water Indians."
  "Adventurers were under
the mind in time,
vines fighting upward
and men thinking
with their hands
behind their backs."
  "There are no teenagers
twisting on smooth maple floors
whose mothers fought battles
with dust
and lust."
  "Only goldfish cows
roaming the meadows of the ocean
  And seagulls asking
when does the tide go out."
  Give the maggot time
and through the frame
of iron fence
the fly will see
the portrait of a city."

# VI

"As an uncle of the unfiltered sun
I throw a handful of dust
into the eyes of old men
leaving thin lines
and scraping the high glaze
of a thunder pot."
  With each handful there is relief
A Methodist fighting with a Jesuit
All emotion is final
and illogical
there is no argument
The greengrocer tells
the plumber's wife
a scallion will never replace
a leek.
  "To insert a bronze key
in a brass lock
does not open the door
nor will articulation
It will open only with a push."

CHORUS:

THE ANSWERS HAVE STOPPED
THE STEEL CLAPPER IS STILL
THERE ARE NO VIBRATIONS
THE KNACKERS HAMMER HAS SLOWED
AND IN ALL OF HELL
                    THERE IS SILENCE

# THE
## POET
### LAUREATE

Who appoints whom?

Loneliness — — —
　　Fantasy — heredity — whimsy — — —

　　　　　　A teacher of light
　　　　　　Harvester of sound
　　　　　　Master of couplet
　　　　　　Or the cutlet?
"Pass the country catsup, if you don't mind, Suh!"

　　Hurry, now, scurry, do not polish clean glasses
There is no time — — —
　　　　Discipline is absent from room six nought nine

A B student has misspelled God
　　　　(She prefers Eliot to Blake)
The bell has been dimmed by bubble gum
The precocious pendulum no longer pushes the stiffening clock.

Scamper and search
　　　　The chessboard corridors
　　　　　　　For henna hair
　　　　　　　　　　And silver sneakers

You are secure in oatmeal and dust
Spanked by a bantum father
And a procession of brown rules
　　　　　　Announced by graceful madmen
　　　　　　and hoary Cassandras

　　　　　　Unproven and forgotten
　　　　　　by starlings and weasles

　　　　　　A middle child dovetrapped
　　　　　　between geology

baptism
and bourbon jugs.

Lyric saint of sibling girls
Poetry cuddled in black tights
Seawashed nipples, feather breasts
Unbuckle your urinary tract
At the command of a poet.

Builder of words and farmhouses
Replete with cold and random fieldstone
To bury a noose of wives.

To rock without rocking
To hide on a white porch
Read to a sterile garden
of onion sprouts
Swap peeps
with a hug of sparrows
Who vanished
into the green genitals
Of a wild walnut tree.

                              C
                               O
                                C
                                 K
                                  E
                                   R
                                    A
                                     L

                Strutting
                Calling
                        Cockle Do Doo Cluck Diddley Doo
in a desecrated farmyard
crow, Chanticleer, coodle
in your untidy ghetto

                        Cinsured by wire
                        electrified and pronged
                        patrolled by patient and bored dogs
                        sentenced to carrying ears for banners
                        and tails for an escutcheon
                        trailed by defeated pratts of brown
                        without grace
                        and beyond your dedicated notice
                        or regal percussion.

            In a land barge prison
            you are indentured slave birds
                        incidentally hatched
                        to toil for survival
                        with a guaranteed wage
                        of corn and millet.
                        With the shrill
                        of a mistcast bell
The cockeral announces,
proclaims
                        the dawn.

Shaking a wax comb
of misshapen scarlet candle

        not yet sturdy and plump
But confident
        of unknown function
With buff quills and amber talons, he slashes
        the pacifist earth
Riffles cloud feathers and tunes
        a toy throat
Trumpets at a suspicious moon
        without the advice of Berlioz
        of the peeping father sun.


He confronts morning

        an inept gymnast rocking
        on a patient startled but eager hen
        Persistent as the black gnat of spring
        a blue and silver bull tuna
Callow
but encouraged
        by the light climb
He displays, pecks and twitches
Mounts, flips and jumps
fumbles and balance

        the cunning and luck
        to transform an egg
        into a day.

# MOAB'S SOLILOQUY

"Why should I come down? Do Gods descend and choose?
For what frailty?"

The certain sure mountain goats clatter from granite
    to suet bellies of soft valleys.
The positive hawk interrupts
the seedy games of busy and bored mice

      WITHIN MY CARCASS OF MYTHOLOGY AND
          PROPHECY
      ANOINTED AND APPOINTED BY A FATHER
          OF ACCURACY
      I AM SECURE WITH THE SPIDER ROOTS OF
          SYCAMORES.

Youthful a ringer of bells, keeper of doves
acrobat in a blue serge village
a sceptic of worn coins courting dandelions
Now a seer and primate of a strange migration
      on a raft of hay in a restless salt sea of horses
      and in seasons of sinking flower boats
      holding tired but sparkling tools
      of a naive and wayward brown generation
      and construct not a pig's hide couch
      or an electric chair, soap box

      A CARPENTER'S SCAFFOLD; A CROSS
Nor a pulpit
carved with seraphims and grapes
but a gantry of words
    SOVEREIGN

      I WILL SELECT WITH A CANDID SCEPTRE
      A MILKWEED STEM FOR A BATON
      TO SNARE RIPPLES AND RHYTHMS OF
      COLOR

Lemons squeezed into the shoes of mother
stride bouyantly among foxglove
to saffron and viney continents

                         Gray keys are not for me
                         I am unawed by innoculation.
                         It is for children in plague years.
Above me in the disguise of a sun
the rose decrees we will meet at four
                         and at no other time.

# MORNING

At dawn
the lemon gull
glides west

To hide
in the sea spreckles
of his green
quilted nest.